Native Americans

Gabrielino

Barbara A. Gray-Kanatiiosh

ABDO Publishing Company

visit us at
www.abdopub.com

Cover Photo: Kayte Deioma
Interior Photos: Kayte Deioma pp. 28, 29, 30
Illustrations: David Kanietakeron Fadden pp. 7, 9, 11, 13, 14, 15, 17, 19, 21, 23, 25, 27
Editors: Kate A. Conley, Jennifer R. Krueger, Kristin Van Cleaf
Art Direction & Maps: Neil Klinepier

Library of Congress Cataloging-in-Publication Data

Gray-Kanatiiosh, Barbara A., 1963-
   Gabrielino / Barbara A. Gray-Kanatiiosh.
     p. cm. -- (Native Americans)
   Summary: An introduction to the history, social life and customs, and present status of the Gabrielino Indians, a tribe whose homelands centered in present day Southern California and included several offshore islands.
   Includes bibliographical references and index.
   ISBN 1-57765-934-1
    1. Gabrielino Indians--Juvenile literature. [1. Gabrielino Indians. 2. Indians of North America--California.]
   I. Title. II. Native Americans (Edina, Minn.)

E99.G15G73 2003
979.4004'9745--dc21

2003048133

About the Author: Barbara A. Gray-Kanatiiosh, JD

Barbara Gray-Kanatiiosh, JD, Ph.D. ABD, is an Akwesasne Mohawk. She resides at the Mohawk Nation and is of the Wolf Clan. She has a Juris Doctorate from Arizona State University, where she was one of the first recipients of ASU's special certificate in Indian Law. Barbara's Ph.D. is in Justice Studies at ASU. She is currently working on her dissertation, which concerns the impacts of environmental injustice on indigenous culture. Barbara works hard to educate children about Native Americans through her writing and Web site, where children may ask questions and receive a written response about the Haudenosaunee culture. The Web site is: www.peace4turtleisland.org

About the Illustrator: David Kanietakeron Fadden

David Kanietakeron Fadden is a member of the Akwesasne Mohawk Wolf Clan. His work has appeared in publications such as *Akwesasne Notes*, *Indian Time*, and the *Northeast Indian Quarterly*. Examples of his work have also appeared in various publications of the Six Nations Indian Museum in Onchiota, NY. His work has also appeared in "How the West Was Lost: Always the Enemy," produced by Gannett Production, which appeared on the Discovery Channel. David's work has been exhibited in Albany, NY; the Lake Placid Center for the Arts; Centre Strathearn in Montreal, Quebec; North Country Community College in Saranac Lake, NY; Paul Smith's College in Paul Smiths, NY; and at the Unison Arts & Learning Center in New Paltz, NY.

Contents

Where They Lived

The Gabrielino (gabriel-eno) called themselves the Tongva (tong-VAH). The name *Tongva* means "People of the Earth" in the Gabrielino language. Their language was a part of the Uto-Aztecan language family.

In the 1500s, Spanish explorers arrived in California and began building **missions**. The Spaniards called the Tongva people San Gabrielino after Mission San Gabriel Arcángel.

This mission was in the Los Angeles Basin, which was part of the Gabrielino's traditional homelands. Their homelands included parts of present-day southern California. They lived near the Chumash, Tataviam, Serrano, and Cahuilla peoples.

Inland, Gabrielino territory stretched from present-day Los Angeles southward to Laguna Beach. The San Gabriel Mountains bordered the land on the east. The Pacific Ocean lay to the west. The Gabrielino homelands also included the islands of Santa Barbara, San Nicolas, San Clemente, and Santa Catalina.

These lands were diverse. They contained **estuaries**, beaches, dunes, grasslands, valleys, and mountains. There were also lakes, rivers, and streams. **Tule** (TOO-lee), shrubs, and willow trees grew in the wetlands. Forests of pine and oak trees grew inland. The islands were home to many types of sea mammals, birds, and plants.

Gabrielino Homelands

5

Society

The Gabrielino lived in villages along the shore. About 200 villages lay within Gabrielino territory. A chief was responsible for a cluster of villages. The chief usually lived in a village at the center of his cluster.

In Gabrielino society, a chief could be a man or a woman. However, chiefdom usually passed from father to son. A chief's duties included protecting the people and keeping peace. A chief also arranged trades and organized group hunts. Chiefs had assistants to help with these duties.

Other members of Gabrielino society also had important roles. Announcers told the people of the chief's decisions. Assistants taught people how to act properly. Messengers traveled among the villages with news of current events. Treasurers collected food and trade goods, which were given to the poor or used at ceremonies.

Medicine people were another important part of society. The Gabrielino believed medicine people were powerful because they spoke with the Creator. Medicine people kept the Gabrielino safe and healthy. They performed ceremonies and healed with herbs. They also divided food after group hunts and gatherings.

A Gabrielino chief advises his people.

Food

The land provided the Gabrielino with food. They hunted, fished, and gathered. They shot deer and foxes with a bow and arrows. Along the shore and on the islands they hunted sea mammals. They used **harpoons** to spear harbor seals, elephant seals, sea lions, sea otters, and dolphins.

The Gabrielino also hunted ground squirrels, rabbits, quail, ducks, geese, and songbirds. The people set out traps, snares, and nets to catch these smaller animals. Sometimes, the Gabrielino smoked rabbits and ground squirrels out of their burrows and clubbed them.

Gabrielino men fished in the ocean for rays, sharks, tuna, and swordfish. The men caught these fish with hook and line, nets, and basket traps. The Gabrielino cut the hooks from **abalone** shells. They made the lines by twisting plant fibers.

The people gathered shellfish such as rock scallops, mussels, clams, abalone, and sea urchins. Women gathered berries, cherries, wild plants, seeds, cattails, piñon nuts, and acorns. The people stored their food in large, woven willow **granaries**.

The Gabrielino ground nuts and seeds into **meal** with a stone mortar and pestle. Acorns were a staple food for the Gabrielino. The people leeched the acorns to remove the **tannic** acid. Then, they ground the acorns into flour. The flour could be made into mush or cakes.

A Gabrielino woman grinds nuts into meal.

Homes

The Gabrielino lived in houses shaped like domes. They built these houses along the coast, with the doors facing the ocean. This way, they avoided the cold north wind. Each home could hold about 50 people. Often three or four families lived inside.

A house's frame was made of willow. To make a frame, the Gabrielino set sapling poles into the ground. The poles formed a circle about 60 feet (18 m) across. The Gabrielino bent the top of the poles over the center of the circle. Next, they tied the poles together with **cordage**. Then, they added cross poles to make the frame sturdier.

For the walls, the Gabrielino tied woven fern and **tule** mats to the frame. At the top of the dome, the people left a hole that could be covered with an animal skin. The hole let in light. It also let out smoke, which came from a fire inside the home. The fire was used for heating the home and cooking food.

Each village also had a sweathouse and a ceremonial enclosure. The people built each sweathouse over a pit. They climbed a ladder to get in and out of the pit.

A ceremonial enclosure was oval, with woven willow walls. Inside, the people painted the frame's poles and hung feathers and flowers. Another ceremonial enclosure was used as a teaching place.

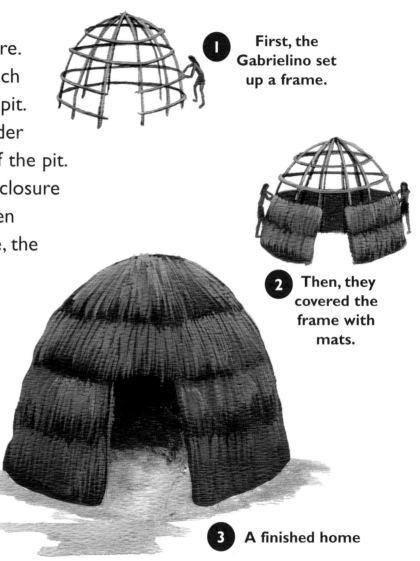

1 First, the Gabrielino set up a frame.

2 Then, they covered the frame with mats.

3 A finished home

Clothing

In the warm California climate, the Gabrielino did not wear much clothing. What clothing they did wear was made with bird skins, animal skins, and plant fibers. The Gabrielino usually went barefoot, but sometimes they wore sandals made of yucca fibers.

Men and women wore capes made of deerskin, rabbit fur, and bird skin. Men also wore **breechcloths** made of deerskin or woven bark. Women wore other clothes, too. They wore aprons made of deerskin or cloth woven from willow or cottonwood bark.

The Gabrielino also wore robes. Robes were created by twisting strips of rabbit fur. Then, the people wove the rabbit fur together with yucca or milkweed fibers. The robes could also be used as blankets.

The Gabrielino had special clothing for ceremonies, too. Ceremonial clothing was brightly colored. It was decorated with feathers, furs, beads, **abalone**, and other shells.

Men and women wore their hair long. They tattooed their faces. The Gabrielino also painted their bodies. The paint consisted of ground minerals mixed with milkweed sap. Women also smeared red **ocher** on their faces. The ocher protected their skin from sunburn and windburn.

A Gabrielino man and woman wear their people's traditional clothing.

Crafts

The Gabrielino were skilled at making crafts. For example, Gabrielino women made feathered capes. They first skinned a bird with a sharp knife. They left the feathers on each skin. Then, they sewed the skins with bone needles and **sinew**.

The Gabrielino had many uses for soapstone. Men could carve bowls, beads, and charms from this stone. It was also used to make cups and pots. Women even used soapstone to bake and cook.

A Gabrielino plank canoe

The Gabrielino also built plank canoes. To build this type of canoe, they first cut redwood planks with stone axes and tools. Next, they drilled the planks and tied them together with **cordage**. Then, the people waterproofed the holes and seams with asphalt.

A Gabrielino craftsman ties canoe planks together.

Canoes were important to the Gabrielino. In canoes, the people traveled to the islands. There, they could find different types of plants and animals. Canoes also helped the Gabrielino to fish and conduct trade.

Family

Gabrielino villages consisted of extended families. Families owned parts of the land. They marked their land by painting the family emblem on a tree or rock. Anyone wanting to hunt, fish, or gather in a family's area first had to ask that family for permission.

Men and women had different tasks. Men hunted, fished, and trapped. Often, men organized group hunts. On these hunts, they traveled inland or out to the islands. Sea mammals and birds were plentiful on San Nicolas Island. Inland the men could fish, or hunt for deer and quail.

Women used digging sticks to unearth edible roots and bulbs. They gathered seeds with seed beater and burden baskets. Seed beater baskets looked like a bird's nest woven on a forked stick. The seed beaters knocked seeds from grass into a bigger burden basket.

Gabrielino women baked on flat pieces of soapstone. They also used soapstone for other types of cooking. For example, they heated fist-size stones in a fire. Then, they placed the stones into a basket to heat water, cook soup, or make mush.

Gabrielino women often made clothing, such as this feathered cape.

17

Children

The Gabrielino loved their children very much. Children were treated with great kindness and respect. Elders helped raise the children. They taught the children and cared for them daily.

The Gabrielino carried their babies in cradle baskets. They wove cradle baskets with **tule** or willow. A cradle basket protected a child while the parents worked.

Older children ran, swam, and played games. One game used a hoop and a pole. The pole was about three feet (1 m) long, and the hoop was about four inches (10 cm) across. The hoop was a willow twig wrapped with buckskin. To play, one child threw the hoop. Then, another child tried to throw the pole through it.

Children learned by watching the adults and helping with daily tasks. For example, Gabrielino girls learned how to make baskets. Besides baskets, they also learned to weave thatch mats. They learned how to prepare rabbit skins and weave them into blankets, too.

Boys also learned practical skills. They learned how to make bows and arrows. In addition, they learned hunting and fishing skills. For example, they learned how to set traps to catch birds.

Gabrielino boys play a game with a hoop and pole.

Myths

The Gabrielino have many stories. One of these stories explains how Earth's land and earthquakes were created.

A long time ago, this world was flooded with water. One day the Creator looked down at all the water and thought, "It is time to make land." The Creator thought, "How am I going to create land in all that water?"

Soon the Creator saw a giant sea turtle swimming along. The Creator called out to Turtle, "Greetings Turtle. I need your help in making land. I would like to build upon your back." Turtle said, "I am happy to help you build land."

The Creator placed mud and dried grass from the Sky World on Turtle's back. The Creator realized he needed more space. The Creator said, "Turtle, call your six brothers. We need their backs, too."

Soon the six turtle brothers arrived. The Creator said, "We need your help. Please line up head to tail facing north to south."

The turtles carry the newly formed land on their backs.

The turtles did as they were asked. The Creator began spreading straw and mud upon their backs. The earth grew.

The turtles began to argue. Some wanted to move east and others west. The turtles moved in opposite directions. They heard a loud snap, and the earth began to shake. Eventually, the turtles made up. But from time to time they still argue or move, and the earth quakes.

War

The Gabrielino were usually a peaceful people, and they did not go to war often. They only fought to settle disputes or to protect their people and lands. Before resorting to warfare, chiefs sent gifts to other villages. The Gabrielino hoped that other villages would become allies rather than enemies.

Sometimes, the villages could resolve their conflict without bloodshed. Instead of going to war, the people of the villages would meet for a song fight. The people sang songs with insults and stomped their feet. Sometimes a song fight would last for over a week.

When the Gabrielino did fight, the chief led the war party. The men went in next, and the women and children followed behind. Women and children carried the supplies and food. In addition, women also picked up shot arrows. They handed the arrows back to the men to reuse.

The Gabrielino wore **tule** armor. Men carried a small knife. They fought with arrows and **sinew**-backed bows. These bows were strong and heavy. For close combat, the men used war clubs. The war club was a carved tree root with sharp, cone-shaped points.

A woman gathers arrows to reuse in a battle.

Contact with Europeans

    The Gabrielino first met Europeans in the 1500s. In 1542, Juan Rodríguez Cabrillo, a Portuguese explorer working for Spain, arrived off the coast of Santa Catalina Island. The Gabrielino canoed out to greet him, and the meeting was peaceful.

    Spaniards visited the Gabrielino again in 1602. That year, Spanish explorer Sebastián Vizcaíno sailed into Gabrielino territory. The Gabrielino greeted him warmly.

    In 1769, Gaspar de Portolá and Father Junípero Serra came to Gabrielino territory. Their arrival forever changed the Gabrielino way of life. The two men planned to build settlements in the area. They built **missions** to convert the native people to Christianity.

    By 1771, four missions had been built. Many Gabrielino were forced to become part of the missionary system. They were not allowed to practice their traditional religion or speak their own language. This destroyed their traditions and way of life.

The **missions** weren't the only problem for the Gabrielino. Native people did not have **immunity** to European illnesses. Many Gabrielino died from smallpox and other sicknesses.

Gaspar de Portolá meets a Gabrielino man.

Toypurina

Toypurina was a respected Gabrielino leader. She was a medicine woman in the 1780s. Her people believed she had supernatural powers.

In 1785, Toypurina and her **apprentice** Nicolas Jose agreed to lead a rebellion against **Mission** San Gabriel Arcángel. They were upset that the missions were causing the Gabrielino to lose their traditional way of life. Many Gabrielino were mistreated at the missions.

In the rebellion, Toypurina convinced six other village clusters to ally with her against the Spaniards. On October 25, Toypurina and other Gabrielino stormed the mission. Toypurina was to kill the priests and soldiers with her magic.

However, the mission had been warned about the rebellion. The missionaries imprisoned Toypurina and the other Gabrielino. Many of the Gabrielino were whipped. Toypurina was sent to another mission in the north, far from her homelands.

Toypurina

 # The Gabrielino Today

It is hard to say how many Gabrielino there are today. Some estimate that there are from 300 to a thousand Gabrielino people. The Gabrielino are not yet **federally recognized**.

About 300 enrolled members belong to the Gabrieleno/Tongva of San Gabriel. The Tribal Council headquarters is in San Gabriel, California, which is part of their traditional homelands. Although the council is not federally recognized, it is recognized by the state of California.

A Gabrielino woman and her sons at the Gabrieleno/Tongva Interpretive Center at Heritage Park in Santa Fe Springs, California

The tribe wants people to realize that the Gabrielino still exist. The people are working hard to restore their **cultural** traditions. For example, retired professor Mark Acuña has helped to create several native gardens. These gardens keep the traditional Gabrielino knowledge of plants alive.

A Gabrielino woman weaves the bottom of a traditional basket with deergrass.

Mark Acuña takes Gabrielino children and adults on a field trip to learn about the uses of native plants.

The Gabrielino also formed a group called the Tongva Dancers. The group preserves the people's dances and songs. The group also teaches others about Gabrielino **culture**. In addition, there is a Tongva village exhibit at Heritage Park in Santa Fe Springs.

Today, the Gabrielino continue to seek **federal recognition**. In 2001, House representative Hilda Solis sponsored a bill called H.R. 2619 to help the Gabrielino receive federal recognition. Becoming federally recognized takes a long time. But, the Gabrielino remain hopeful that they will soon receive the recognition they are seeking.

A member of the Tongva Dancers sets his headdress in place before a dance at a Gabrielino gathering.

Glossary

abalone - edible, spineless animals that cling to rocks.

apprentice - a person who learns a trade or craft from a skilled worker.

breechcloth - a piece of hide or cloth, usually worn by men, that wraps between the legs and ties with a belt around the waist.

cordage - ropes or cords made by twisting plant fibers.

culture - the customs, arts, and tools of a nation or people at a certain time.

estuary - the body of water where a river's current meets an ocean's tide.

federal recognition - the U.S. government's recognition of a tribe as being an independent nation. The tribe is then eligible for special funding and for protection of its reservation lands.

granary - a building used for storing grain.

harpoon - a spear made from wood or bone used to kill seals, walrus, and whales.

immunity - protection against disease.

meal - coarsely ground seeds.

mission - a center or headquarters for religious work.

ocher - a red or yellow iron ore used for color.

sinew - a band of tough fibers that joins a muscle to a bone.

tannic - related to tannin, a bitter tasting yellow or brown mix of chemicals.

tule - a type of reed that grows in wetlands. Tule is native to California.

Web Sites

To learn more about the Gabrielino, visit ABDO Publishing Company on the World Wide Web at **www.abdopub.com**. Web sites about the Gabrielino are featured on our Book Links page. These links are routinely monitored and updated to provide the most current information available.

Index

A
Acuña, Mark 29

C
Cabrillo, Juan Rodríguez 24
Cahuilla Indians 4
California 4, 12, 28
ceremonies 6, 7, 11, 12
chiefs 6, 22
children 18, 19, 22
Chumash Indians 4
clothing 12
cradle baskets 18
crafts 14, 18

D
diseases 25

E
elders 18
Europeans 4, 24, 25, 26

F
family 6, 10, 16, 17, 18
federal recognition 28, 30

fishing 8, 15, 16, 19
food 6, 7, 8, 9, 10, 17, 22

G
games 18
gathering 7, 8, 9, 16

H
homelands 4, 5, 6, 16, 22, 24, 26, 28
homes 10
hunting 6, 7, 8, 16, 19

J
Jose, Nicolas 26

L
language 4, 24

M
medicine people 7, 26
Mission San Gabriel Arcángel 4, 26
missions 4, 24, 25, 26

P
plank canoes 15
Portolá, Gaspar de 24

S
Serra, Junípero 24
Serrano Indians 4
Solis, Hilda 30
stories 20, 21
sweathouse 11

T
Tataviam Indians 4
tattoos 13
tools 8, 9, 10, 14, 15, 16, 17, 19
Toypurina 26
trading 6, 15

V
villages 6, 11, 16, 22, 26
Vizcaíno, Sebastián 24

W
war 22, 23
weapons 22, 23